Knit a Doze
slippers

Designs by Amy Polcyn

HOUSE of
WHITE
BIRCHES

PUBLISHERS
SINCE 1947

Table of Contents

Cable Clog Slippers,
page 31

Ruggedly Warm Loafers,
page 37

Fair Isle Boots,
page 13

Red Sports Cars,
page 4

General Instructions

Sizing

Each size category (Child, Woman, Man) includes 3 length options (small, medium, large). If a custom length is desired, simply work the foot until it measures approximately 2 inches less than desired length before working toe (or heel, on toe-up patterns). Slippers are stretchy and forgiving, so don't worry if your foot is a bit wider (or narrower) than slipper.

Sizing is as follows:

Child: 5–6 inch foot circumference
   Small = shoe sizes 8–10 = 6-inch foot length
   Medium = shoe sizes 11–13 = 7-inch foot length
   Large = shoe sizes 1–3 = 8-inch foot length

Woman: 7–8 inch foot circumference
   Small = shoe sizes 5–7 = 9-inch foot length
   Medium = shoe sizes 8–10 = 10-inch foot length
   Large = shoe sizes 11–13 = 11-inch foot length

Man: 9–10 inch foot circumference
   Small = shoe sizes 7–9 = 10-inch foot length
   Medium = shoe sizes 10–12 = 11-inch foot length
   Large = shoe sizes 13+ = 12-inch foot length

Needles

Most patterns in this book call for double-point needles. In some cases, it is to accommodate working in the round (feel free to use the Magic Loop or 2 circulars if you prefer), and in other cases they are used simply to make it easier to work back in forth in rows on small numbers of sts (in which case, use just 2 of the needles as straights). For I-cord and applied I-cord, 2 double-point needles are required.

Special Abbreviations

K3tog: Knit 3 sts tog
K1-tbl: Knit st through the back loop
C4B: Slip 2 sts to cable needle and hold to back, k2, k2 from cable needle
C4F: Slip 2 sts to cable needle and hold to front, k2, k2 from cable needle

Special Techniques

Wrap and Turn (W/T): Work to stitch indicated. Bring yarn between needles to front of work (or back, if already on front). Slip next stitch purlwise. Return yarn to original position. Slip wrapped stitch back to left needle without knitting or purling it, turn.

Pick up wrap: Work to wrapped stitch. With tip of needle, lift wrap onto left needle (from the right side on knit rows and from the wrong side on purl rows). Knit (or purl) next stitch together with wrap.

I-cord: Cast on 4 sitches on a double-point needle. *Slide stitches to opposite end of needle, knit 4, do not turn; repeat from * until cord is desired length. Bind off.

Applied I-cord: Cast on 4 stitches on a double-point needle. Work 1 row of I-cord, and with wrong side facing, pick up 1 more stitch from edge of piece for 5 stitches. *Knit 3, knit 2 together (last stitch on needle and picked-up stitch), pick up and knit another stitch from edge of piece; repeat from * around. Skip stitches on pick-up round/row as needed to keep edge from flaring. Bind off and sew or graft using Kitchener stitch to opposite end of cord.

Kitchener Stitch: Hold needles parallel with yarn coming from back needle. Thread yarn on a tapestry needle. To begin, insert yarn in first stitch on front needle purlwise, then in first stitch on back needle knitwise.

   Step 1: Insert yarn through first stitch on front needle knitwise and take stitch off needle, insert yarn through next stitch on front needle purlwise.

   Step 2: Insert yarn through first stitch on back needle purlwise and take stitch off needle, insert yarn through next stitch on back needle knitwise.

   Repeat Steps 1 and 2 until 2 stitches remain. Insert yarn through stitch on front needle knitwise and take off needle, insert yarn through stitch on back needle purlwise and take off needle. Fasten off end. ❖

Red Sports Cars

Design by Amy Polcyn

Skill Level

 INTERMEDIATE

Sizes

Child's small (medium, large) Fits shoe size 8–10 (11–13, 1–3) Instructions are given for smallest size, with larger sizes in parentheses. When only 1 number is given, it applies to all sizes.

Finished Measurement

Length: 6 (7, 8) inches

Materials

- Plymouth Encore Worsted (worsted weight; 75% acrylic/25% wool; 200 yds/100g per ball): 1 ball red #174 (MC) and small amount each of black #217 (A) and yellow #215 (B)
- Size 8 (5mm) double-point needles or size needed to obtain gauge
- Stitch markers or small safety pins

Gauge

20 sts and 32 rows = 4 inches/10 cm in garter st. To save time, take time to check gauge.

Special Technique

Wrap and Turn (W/T): Work to st indicated, bring yarn between needles to front of work, slip next st to RH needle, take yarn to back, slip wrapped st back to LH needle, turn, leaving rem sts unworked.

Pattern Notes

Two double-point needles are used to work back and forth in rows on the smaller number of stitches used for the heel, foot and toe of slippers.

Two double-point needles are used to work the applied I-cord top edge and I-cord wheels.

Slipper

With MC, cast on 15 sts.

Heel

Work garter st short-row heel as follows:

Rows 1 (RS) and 2: Knit to last st, W/T.

Note: Mark Row 1 as RS.

Rows 3 and 4: Knit to last 2 sts, W/T.

Rows 5 and 6: Knit to last 3 sts, W/T.

Rows 7 and 8: Knit to last 4 sts, W/T.

Note: There are now 4 wrapped sts at each end of row and 7 unwrapped sts in the center.

Rows 9 and 10: Knit to first wrapped st (4th st from end of row), knit this st, turn.

Rows 11 and 12: Knit to next wrapped st, knit this st, turn.

Continue until all wrapped sts have been worked.

Foot

Work even in garter st until piece measures 4 (5, 6) inches.

Note: Measure length in center of row.

Toe & toe flap

Work same as heel until all wrapped sts have been worked. Place small safety pin or marker in center of last row.

Work even in garter st until toe flap measures 1½ (2, 2½) inches from safety pin. Bind off.

Sew sides of toe flap to sides of foot.

Applied I-cord edge

With MC, cast on 4 sts, slide sts to opposite end of needle, pulling yarn across back of work, k4. Beg at center back of heel with RS facing, pick up and knit 1 st along edge of slipper—5 sts.

Work applied I-cord as follows:

*K3, k2tog (last st on needle and picked up st), pick up and knit another st from edge of slipper; rep from * around, skipping a row along edge of slipper when picking up sts as needed to keep edge flat.

Graft sts to cast on sts using Kitchener st *or* bind off sts and sew ends tog.

Wheel
Make 4 per slipper

With A, cast on 4 sts, *slide sts to opposite end of needle, pull yarn across back of work, k4; rep from * until I-cord measures 2½ inches.

Fold into a circle. Graft sts to cast-on sts using Kitchener st or bind off and sew ends tog.

Finishing
Referring to photo, sew wheels on slipper. With B, embroider several straight sts in center of each wheel for hubcap. ❖

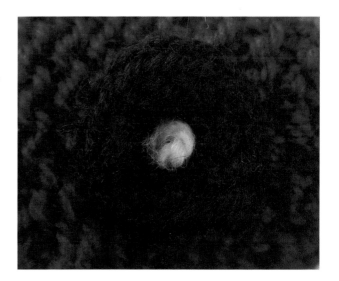

Little Jane Slippers

Design by Amy Polcyn

Skill Level

 ◼◼◻◻ **EASY**

Sizes

Child's small (medium, large) Fits shoe size 8–10 (11–13, 1–3) Instructions are given for smallest size, with larger sizes in parentheses. When only 1 number is given, it applies to all sizes.

Finished Measurement

Length: 6 (7, 8) inches

Materials

- Universal Classic Chunky Long Print (chunky weight; 75% acrylic/25% wool; 131 yds/100g per skein): 1 skein indigo blues #6311
- Size 9 (5.5mm) double-point needles
- Size 10 (6mm) double-point needles or size needed to obtain gauge
- Stitch markers
- 2 (⅞-inch) buttons

House of White Birches, Berne, Indiana 46711   AnniesAttic.com

Gauge

14 sts and 28 rows = 4 inches/10 cm in garter st with larger needles.
To save time, take time to check gauge.

Special Technique

Wrap and Turn (W/T): Work to st indicated, bring yarn between needles to front of work, slip next st to RH needle, take yarn to back, slip wrapped st back to LH needle, turn.

Pattern Notes

Two double-point needles are used to work back and forth in rows on the smaller number of stitches used for the heel, foot and toe of slippers.

Top edge is worked in rounds with the set of double-point needles.

Slipper

With larger needles, cast on 11 sts.

Heel

Work garter st short-row heel as follows:

Rows 1 (RS) and 2: Knit to last st, W/T.

Note: Mark Row 1 as RS.

Rows 3 and 4: Knit to last 2 sts, W/T.

Rows 5 and 6: Knit to last 3 sts, W/T.

Note: There are now 3 wrapped sts at each end of row and 5 unwrapped sts in the center.

Rows 7 and 8: Knit to first wrapped st (3rd st from end of row), knit this st, turn.

Rows 9 and 10: Knit to next wrapped st, knit this st, turn.

Continue until all wrapped sts have been worked.

Foot

Work even until piece measures 4 (5, 6) inches.

Note: Measure length in center of row.

Toe

Work same as heel until all wrapped sts have been worked. Bind off.

Top Edge

With smaller needles and beg at center back of heel, pick up and knit 44 (50, 56) sts evenly spaced. Divide onto needles. Place marker and join to work in rnds.

Rnd 1: Purl, dec 3 sts evenly across top of toe— 41 (47, 53) sts.

Rnd 2: Knit.

Rnd 3: Purl.

Bind off kwise.

Strap

Mark desired location of strap along side of top edge. With smaller needles pick up and knit 3 sts at marker along side edge of slipper. Work in garter st, slipping the first st of each row pwise, until strap measures 3 inches.

Next row (buttonhole): K2tog, yo, k1.

Work 1 row even. Bind off.

Work strap for 2nd slipper to mirror first slipper.

Sew button opposite buttonhole. ❖

Ballerina Slippers

Design by Amy Polcyn

Skill Level

 INTERMEDIATE

Sizes

Child's small (medium, large) Fits shoe size 8–10 (11–13, 1–3) Instructions are given for smallest size, with larger sizes in parentheses. When only 1 number is given, it applies to all sizes.

Finished Measurement

Length: 6 (7, 8) inches

Materials

- Nashua Handknits Grand Opera; (DK weight; 86% wool/9%viscose/ 5% metallized polyester; 128 yds/50g per ball): 1 ball dusty pink #8559
- Size 5 (3.75mm) double-point needles or size needed to obtain gauge
- Small safety pin or stitch marker

Gauge

24 sts and 32 rows = 4 inches/10cm in St st.
To save time, take time to check gauge.

Pattern Notes

Two double-point needles are used to work back and forth in rows on the smaller number of stitches used for the toe, foot and heel of slippers.

The top edging can be worked in single crochet instead of Applied I-cord, if desired.

Slipper

Cast on 20 sts.

Toe

Work origami toe as follows:

Row 1 (RS): Sl 1p, knit to last st, turn.

Row 2: Sl 1p, purl to last st, turn.

Row 3: Sl 1p, knit to last 2 sts, turn.

Row 4: Sl 1p, purl to last 2 sts, turn.

Row 5: Sl 1p, knit to last 3 sts, turn.

Row 6: Sl 1p, purl to last 3 sts, turn.

Row 7: Sl 1p, knit to last 4 sts, turn.

Row 8: Sl 1p, purl to last 4 sts, turn.

Row 9: Sl 1p, knit to last 5 sts, turn.

Row 10: Sl 1p, purl to last 5 sts, turn.

Row 11: Sl 1p, knit to last 6 sts, turn.

Row 12: Sl 1p, purl to last 6 sts, turn. Place small safety pin or marker on st in center of row.

Note: There are now 6 unworked sts at each end and 8 sts in the center.

Next row (RS): Sl 1p, knit to last 6 sts, pick up st from row below (as for a lifted increase) and work as ssk tog with next st on needle.

Next row: Sl 1p, purl to last 6 sts, pick up st from row below and p2tog with next st on needle.

Next row: Sl 1p, knit to last 5 sts, pick up st from row below and ssk tog with next st on needle.

Next row: Sl 1p, purl to last 5 sts, pick up st from row below and p2tog with next st on needle.

Continue as established until all sts have been worked.

Foot

Work even in St st until piece measures 4 (5, 6) inches from safety pin.

Heel

Work same as toe until all unworked sts have been worked. Bind off.

Applied I-cord edge

Cast on 4 sts, slide sts to opposite end of needle, pulling yarn across back of work, k4. Beg at center back of heel with RS facing, pick up and knit 1 st along edge of slipper—5 sts.

Work applied I-cord as follows:

*K3, k2tog (last st on needle and picked up st), pick up and knit another st from edge of slipper; rep from * around top edge, skipping a row of slipper when picking up sts as needed to keep edge flat.

Graft sts to cast-on sts using Kitchener st or bind off sts and sew ends tog.

Tie
Make 2 per slipper

Cast on 4 sts, *slide sts to opposite end of needle, pull yarn across back of work, k4; rep from * until I-cord measures 21 inches. Slide sts to opposite end of needle, pull yarn across back of work and bind off.

Finishing
Sew end of tie to each side of slipper. Cross ties over foot, wrap around ankle and tie. ❖

Fair Isle Boots

Design by Amy Polcyn

Skill Level

◼◼◼▢ INTERMEDIATE

Sizes

Woman's small (medium, large) To fit shoe size 5–7 (8–10, 11–13) Instructions are given for smallest size, with larger sizes in parentheses. When only 1 number is given, it applies to all sizes.

Finished Measurement

Length: 9 (10, 11) inches

Materials

- Cascade 220 Wool (worsted weight; 100% wool; 220 yds/100g per skein): 1 (2, 2) skeins lagoon #7812 (A) and 1 skein each mint #9076 (B) and duck-egg blue #9427 (C)
- Size 7 (4.5mm) set of 4 double-point needles or size needed to obtain gauge
- Size G/6 (4mm) crochet hook
- Stitch marker
- 1¼-inch piece of cardboard or small pompom maker

4 MEDIUM

14

Gauge

20 sts and 28 rows = 4 inches/10 cm in St st.
To save time, take time to check gauge.

Special Abbreviation

N1, N2, N3: Needle 1, Needle 2, Needle 3

Pattern Stitch

See Color Chart.

Pattern Note

When stranding unused yarns on wrong side of work, be certain to strand them very loosely to avoid making leg of boot too tight.

Boot

Cuff

With A, cast on 40 sts. Divide sts among N1, N2 and N3. Place marker and join, being careful not to twist the sts.

Next rnd: *K2, p2; rep from * around.

Rep last rnd until rib measures 6 inches.

Next rnd (eyelet): *K2, k2tog, yo; rep from * around.

Leg

Work in St st until piece measures 1 inch from end of rib.

Work Rnds 1–18 of Color Chart. Cut B and C. Work even in St st with A until piece measures 10½ inches from cast-on edge.

Heel Flap

Work on 20 heel sts only; leave rem 20 instep sts on hold.

Row 1 (RS): *Sl 1p, k1; rep from * across.

Row 2: Sl 1p, purl to end.

Rep [Rows 1 and 2] 9 times.

Turn Heel

Row 1 (RS): K12, ssk, k1, turn.

Row 2: Sl 1p, p5, p2tog, p1, turn.

Row 3: Sl 1p, knit to 1 st before gap, ssk (1 stitch from each side of gap), k1, turn.

Row 4: Sl 1p, purl to 1 st before gap, p2tog (1 stitch from each side of gap), p1, turn.

Rep Rows 3 and 4 until all sts have been worked, ending with a WS row—12 sts.

Gusset

N1: Knit heel sts, pick up and knit 10 sts along side of heel flap; N2: work in St st across instep sts; N3: pick up and knit 10 sts along opposite side of heel flap, k6 heel sts from N1 onto N3—20 instep sts and 32 heel sts.

Note: Beg of rnd is at center back of heel.

Rnd 1: N1: Knit to last 3 heel sts, k2tog, k1; N2: knit instep sts; N3: K1, ssk, knit to end of round—50 sts.

Rnd 2: Knit.

Rep [Rnds 1 and 2] 5 times—40 sts.

Foot

Work even until foot measures 7 (8, 9) inches from back of heel.

Toe

Rnd 1: N1: Knit to last 3 heel sts, k2tog, k1; N2: K1, ssk, knit to last 3 sts, k2tog, k1; N3: K1, ssk, knit to end of rnd—36 sts.

Rnd 2: Knit.

Rep [Rnds 1 and 2] 7 times—8 sts rem.

Place 4 sts on one needle and 4 on other and graft toe using Kitchener stitch.

Tie

With crochet hook and C, work a chain 28 inches long. Fasten off. Using cardboard or pompom maker and B and C held tog, make 2 pompoms. Weave tie through eyelet row on boot, sew pompom to each end. Tie ends in bow.

Fold cuff down. ❖

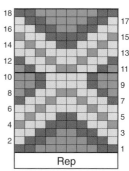

COLOR CHART

STITCH & COLOR KEY
- With lagoon (A), k on RS, p on WS
- With mint (B), k on RS, p on WS
- With duck-egg blue (C), k on RS, p on WS

Ballet Flats

Design by Amy Polcyn

Skill Level

 INTERMEDIATE

Sizes

Woman's small (medium, large) Fits shoe size 5–7 (8–10, 11–13) Instructions are given for smallest size, with larger sizes in parentheses. When only 1 number is given, it applies to all sizes.

Finished Measurement

Length: 9 (10, 11) inches

Materials

- Caron Simply Soft Eco (worsted weight; 80% acrylic/20% NatureSpun™ recycled polyester 5 oz/249 yds per ball): 1 ball plum perfect #0032
- Size 7 (4.5mm) double-point needles or size needed to obtain gauge
- Small safety pin or stitch marker
- 1 yd ¼-inch-wide satin ribbon

Gauge

20 sts and 24 rows = 4 inches/10cm in St st.
To save time, take time to check gauge.

Pattern Notes

Two double-point needles are used to work back and forth in rows on the smaller number of stitches used for the toe, foot and heel of slippers.

The top edging can be worked in single crochet, if desired, instead of Applied I-cord.

Slipper

Cast on 20 sts.

Work in St st for 1 inch.

Toe

Continue in St st, working origami toe as follows:

Row 1 (RS): Sl 1p, knit to last st, turn.

Row 2: Sl 1p, purl to last st, turn.

Row 3: Sl 1p, knit to last 2 sts, turn.

Row 4: Sl 1p, purl to last 2 sts, turn.

Row 5: Sl 1p, knit to last 3 sts, turn.

Row 6: Sl 1p, purl to last 3 sts, turn.

Row 7: Sl 1p, knit to last 4 sts, turn.

Row 8: Sl 1p, purl to last 4 sts, turn.

Row 9: Sl 1p, knit to last 5 sts, turn.

Row 10: Sl 1p, purl to last 5 sts, turn.

Row 11: Sl 1p, knit to last 6 sts, turn.

Row 12: Sl 1p, purl to last 6 sts, turn. Place small safety pin or marker in center of row.

Note: There are now 6 unworked sts at each end and 8 sts in the center.

Next row (RS): Sl 1p, knit to last 6 sts, pick up st from row below (as for a lifted increase) and work as ssk tog with next st on needle.

Next row: Sl 1p, purl to last 6 sts, pick up st from row below and p2tog with next st on needle.

Next row: Sl 1p, knit to last 5 sts, pick up st from row below and ssk tog with next st on needle.

Next row: Sl 1p, purl to last 5 sts, pick up st from row below and p2tog with next st on needle.

Continue as established until all sts have been worked.

Foot

Work even in St st until piece measures 7 (8, 9) inches from safety pin.

Heel

Work same as toe until all sts have been worked. Bind off.

Sew sides of toe flap to sides of slipper.

Applied I-cord edge

Cast on 4 sts, slide sts to opposite end of needle, pulling yarn across back of work, k4. Beg at center back of heel with RS facing, pick up and knit 1 st along edge of slipper—5 sts.

Work applied I-cord as follows:

*K3, k2tog (last st on needle and picked up st), pick up and knit another st from edge of slipper; rep from * around top edge, skipping a row along edge of slipper when picking up sts as needed to keep edge flat.

Graft sts to cast-on sts using Kitchener st *or* bind off sts and sew ends tog.

Finishing
Cut ribbon in half, and weave through center sts at toe and tie in bow. Trim ends. ❖

Brightly Beaded Moccasins

Design by Amy Polcyn

Skill Level

▰▰▰▱ INTERMEDIATE

Sizes

Woman's small (medium, large) Fits shoe size 5–7 (8–10, 11–13) Instructions are given for smallest size, with larger sizes in parentheses. When only 1 number is given, it applies to all sizes.

Finished Measurement

Length: 9 (10, 11) inches

Materials

- Mission Falls 1824 Wool (worsted weight; 100% wool; 85 yds/50g per ball): 2 balls poppy #011 (MC) and 1 ball thyme #016 (CC)
- Size 7 (4.5mm) double-point needles or size needed to obtain gauge
- Stitch marker
- Beading needle
- Matching sewing thread
- Size 6/0 E beads to match both colors of yarn (24 cranberry and 72 green)

Gauge

18 sts and 24 rows = 4 inches/10cm in St st.
To save time, take time to check gauge.

Special Technique

Wrap and Turn (W/T): Work to st indicated, *on RS rows*, bring yarn between needles to front of work, slip next st to RH needle, take yarn to back, slip wrapped st back to LH needle and turn; *on WS rows*, take yarn between needles to back, slip next st to RH needle, bring yarn between needles to front, slip wrapped st back to LH needle and turn.

Pattern Stitch
See Color Chart.

Pattern Notes
Beads are sewn in place after slipper is finished with beading needle and thread.

Two double-point needles are used to work back and forth in rows on the smaller number of stitches used for the heel, foot and toe of slippers.

Top edge is worked in rounds with the set of double-point needles.

Slipper
With MC, cast on 18 sts.

Heel
Work short-row heel in St st as follows:

Row 1 (RS): Knit to last st, W/T.

Row 2: Purl to last st, W/T.

Row 3: Knit to last 2 sts, W/T.

Row 4: Purl to last 2 sts, W/T.

Row 5: Knit to last 3 sts, W/T.

Row 6: Purl to last 3 sts, W/T.

Row 7: Knit to last 4 sts, W/T.

Row 8: Purl to last 4 sts, W/T.

Row 9: Knit to last 5 sts, W/T.

Row 10: Purl to last 5 sts, W/T.

Note: There are 5 wrapped sts at each end of row and 8 unwrapped sts in the center.

Row 11: Sl 1p, knit to first wrapped st (5th stitch from end of row), lift wrap and knit tog with wrapped st, turn.

Row 12: Sl 1p, purl to first wrapped st (5th stitch from end of row), lift wrap and purl tog with wrapped st, turn.

Row 13: Sl 1p, knit to wrapped st, lift wrap and knit tog with wrapped st, turn.

Row 14: Sl 1p, purl to wrapped st, lift wrap and purl tog with wrapped st, turn.

Continue in same manner until all wrapped sts have been worked.

Foot
Work even in St st until piece measures 7 (8, 9) inches.

Toe
Work same as heel.

Work Rows 1–14 of Color Chart, stranding color not in use loosely on WS.

Finishing
Sew beads in place, matching colors and following chart.

Sew sides of toe to sides of slipper.

Top Edge
With RS facing and beg at center back with MC, pick up and knit 52 (60, 68) sts around top edge. Divide sts on needles, place marker and join to work in rnds.

Rnd 1: Purl.

Rnd 2: Knit.

Rnd 3: Purl.

Bind off kwise. ❖

STITCH & COLOR KEY
■ With MC, k on RS, p on WS
■ With CC, k on RS, p on WS
B Sew bead over st, matching color (CC bead over CC sts)

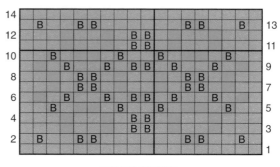

COLOR CHART

Mary Jane Slippers

Design by Amy Polcyn

Skill level

■ ■ □ □ EASY

Sizes

Woman's small (medium, large) Fits shoe size 5–7 (8–10, 11–13) Instructions are given for smallest size, with larger sizes in parentheses. When only 1 number is given, it applies to all sizes.

Finished Measurement

Length: 9 (10, 11) inches

Materials

- Universal Classic Chunky Long Print (chunky weight; 75% acrylic/25% wool; 131 yds/100g per skein): 1 skein green meadow #6313
- Size 9 (5.5mm) double-point needles
- Size 10 (6mm) double-point needles or size needed to obtain gauge
- Stitch markers
- 2 (⅞-inch) buttons

Gauge

14 sts and 28 rows = 4 inches/10cm in garter st with larger needles.
To save time, take time to check gauge.

Special Technique

Wrap and Turn (W/T): Work to st indicated, bring yarn between needles to front of work, slip next st to RH needle, take yarn to back, slip wrapped st back to LH needle, turn.

Pattern Notes

Two double-point needles are used to work back and forth in rows on the smaller number of stitches used for the heel, foot and toes of these slippers.

Top edge is worked in rounds with the set of double-point needles.

Slipper

With larger needles, cast on 13 sts.

Heel

Work garter st short-row heel as follows:

Rows 1 (RS) and 2: Knit to last st, W/T.

Note: Mark Row 1 as RS.

Rows 3 and 4: Knit to last 2 sts, W/T.

Rows 5 and 6: Knit to last 3 sts, W/T.

Rows 7 and 8: Knit to last 4 sts, W/T.

Note: There are now 4 wrapped sts at each end of row and 5 unwrapped sts in the center.

Rows 9 and 10: Knit to first wrapped st (4th stitch from end of row), knit this st, turn.

Rows 11 and 12: Knit to next wrapped st, knit this st, turn.

Continue until all wrapped sts have been worked.

Foot

Work even until piece measures 7 (8, 9) inches.

Note: Measure length in center of row.

Toe

Work same as heel until all wrapped sts have been worked. Bind off.

Top Edge

Beg at center back heel with smaller needles, pick up and knit 65 (71, 77) sts. Divide on needles. Place marker and join to work in rnds.

Rnd 1: Purl, dec 3 sts across top of toe— 62 (68, 74) sts.

Rnd 2: Knit.

Rnd 3: Purl.

Bind off kwise.

Strap

Mark desired location of strap along side of top edge. With smaller needles, pick up and knit 3 sts at marker along side edge of slipper. Work in garter st, slipping the first st of each row pwise, until strap measures 3½ inches.

Next row (buttonhole): K2tog, yo, k1.

Knit 1 row. Bind off.

Work strap for 2nd slipper to mirror first.

Sew button opposite buttonhole. ❖

Lacy Toe-Up Slipper Socks

Design by Amy Polcyn

Skill Level

 INTERMEDIATE

Sizes

Woman's small (medium, large) Fits shoe size 5–7 (8–10, 11–13) Instructions are given for smallest size, with larger sizes in parentheses. When only 1 number is given, it applies to all sizes.

Finished Measurement

Length: 9 (10, 11) inches

Materials

- Plymouth Yarn Galway Chunky (chunky weight; 100% wool; 123 yds/100g per ball): 3 skeins green #750
- Size 11 (8mm) double-point needles (set of 5) or size needed to obtain gauge
- Size J/10 (6mm) crochet hook
- Stitch marker

Gauge

12 sts and 14 rows = 4 inches/10cm in St st.
To save time, take time to check gauge.

Special Technique

Wrap and Turn (W/T): Work to st indicated, *on RS rows*, bring yarn between needles to front of work, slip next st to RH needle, take yarn around st to back, slip wrapped st back to LH needle and turn; *on WS rows*, take yarn between needles to back, slip next st to RH needle, bring yarn between needles around st to front, slip wrapped st back to LH needle and turn.

Pattern Stitch

Lace Pattern (multiple of 12 sts)

Rnd 1: Knit.

Rnd 2: Purl.

Rnds 3 and 4: Rep Rnds 1 and 2.

Rnd 5: *[K2tog] twice, [yo, k1] 3 times, yo, [ssk] twice, k1; rep from * around.

Rnd 6: Knit.

Rnds 7–12: Rep [Rnds 5 and 6] 3 times.

Rep Rnds 1–12 for pat.

House of White Birches, Berne, Indiana 46711 AnniesAttic.com

Slipper Sock

With waste yarn and crochet hook, ch 14. Fasten off. With project yarn and needles, pick up and knit 12 sts from ch, working 1 st in back "bump" of each ch and leaving 1 ch on each end unworked.

Purl 1 row.

Toe

Row 1 (RS): Knit to last st, W/T.

Row 2: Purl to last st, W/T.

Row 3: Knit to last 2 sts W/T.

Row 4: Purl to last 2 sts, W/T.

Row 5: Knit to last 3 sts, W/T.

Row 6: Purl to last 3 sts, W/T.

Row 7: Knit to last 4 sts, W/T.

Row 8: Purl to last 4 sts, W/T.

Note: There are 4 wrapped sts at each end of row and 4 unwrapped sts in the center.

Row 9: Sl 1p, knit to first wrapped st (4th stitch from end of row), lift wrap and knit tog with wrapped st, turn.

Row 10: Sl 1p, purl to first wrapped st (4th stitch from end of row), lift wrap and purl tog with wrapped st, turn.

Row 11: Sl 1p, knit to wrapped st, lift wrap and knit tog with wrapped st, turn.

Row 12: Sl 1p, purl to wrapped st, lift wrap and purl tog with wrapped st, turn.

Continue in same manner until all wrapped sts have been worked.

Divide sts onto 2 double-point needles.

Undo crochet chain and divide "live" sts between 2 additional double-point needles. Place marker and join to work in rnds—24 sts.

Note: It may be necessary to pick up a st at one end of the "live" sts in order to have 24 sts on the needles.

Foot

Work even in St st until foot measures 7 (8, 9) inches.

Heel

Place 12 sole sts on 1 needle for heel and work same as toe on these sts only until all wrapped sts are worked.

Divide heel sts onto 2 needles. Join to work cuff in rnds.

Cuff

Work even in St st on all sts for 1 inch.

Turn with WS facing, (to allow RS of Lace pat to show when cuff is folded down) and work in Lace pat until cuff measures 7 inches. Bind off very loosely.

Fold cuff down. ❖

Ribbed Toe-Up Slipper Socks

Design by Amy Polcyn

Skill Level

■ ■ ■ ▢ INTERMEDIATE

Sizes

Man's small (medium, large) Fits shoe sizes 7–9 (10–12, 13+) Instructions are given for smallest size, with larger sizes in parentheses. When only 1 number is given, it applies to all sizes.

Finished Measurement

Length: 10 (11, 12) inches

Materials

- Plymouth Yarn Cleckheaton Country 8 Ply (chunky weight; 100% wool; 105 yds/50g per ball): 3 (3, 4) balls gray #2292
- Size 11 (8mm) set of 5 double-point needles or size needed to obtain gauge
- Size J/10 (6mm) crochet hook
- Stitch marker

Gauge

12 sts and 14 rows = 4 inches/10cm in St st.
To save time, take time to check gauge.

Special Technique

Wrap and Turn (W/T): Work to st indicated, *on RS rows*, bring yarn between needles to front of work, slip next st to RH needle, take yarn around st to back, slip wrapped st back to LH needle and turn; *on WS rows*, take yarn between needles to back, slip next st to RH needle, bring yarn between needles around st to front, slip wrapped st back to LH needle and turn.

Slipper Sock

With waste yarn and crochet hook, ch 16. Fasten off. With project yarn and needles, pick up and knit 14 sts from ch, working 1 st in back "bump" of each ch and leaving 1 ch on each end unworked.

Purl 1 row.

Toe

Row 1 (RS): Knit to last st, W/T.

Row 2: Purl to last st, W/T.

Row 3: Knit to last 2 sts W/T.

Row 4: Purl to last 2 sts, W/T.

Row 5: Knit to last 3 sts, W/T.

Row 6: Purl to last 3 sts, W/T.

Row 7: Knit to last 4 sts, W/T.

Row 8: Purl to last 4 sts, W/T.

Note: There are 4 wrapped sts at each end of row and 6 unwrapped sts in the center.

Row 9: Sl 1p, knit to first wrapped st (4th stitch from end of row), lift wrap and knit tog with wrapped st, turn.

Row 10: Sl 1p, purl to first wrapped st (4th stitch from end of row), lift wrap and purl tog with wrapped st, turn.

Row 11: Sl 1p, knit to wrapped st, lift wrap and knit tog with wrapped st, turn.

Row 12: Sl 1p, purl to wrapped st, lift wrap and purl tog with wrapped st, turn.

Continue as established until all wrapped sts have been worked.

Divide sts onto 2 double-point needles.

Undo crochet ch and divide "live" sts between 2 additional double-point needles. Place marker and join in to work in rnds—28 sts.

Note: It may be necessary to pick up a st at one end of the "live" sts in order to have 28 sts on the needles.

Foot

Work even in St st until foot measures 8 (9, 10) inches.

Heel

Place 14 sole sts on 1 needle for heel and work same as toe on these sts only until all wrapped sts are worked.

Divide heel sts onto 2 needles. Join to work cuff in rnds.

Cuff

Work even in St st on all sts for 1 inch.

Next rnd: *K2, p2; rep from * around.

Rep last rnd until cuff measures 7 inches. Bind off very loosely in pat.

Fold cuff down. ❖

Cable Clog Slippers

Design by Amy Polcyn

Skill Level

 ■■□□ EASY

Sizes

Woman's small (medium, large) Fits shoe size 5–7 (8–10, 11–13) Instructions are given for smallest size, with larger sizes in parentheses. When only 1 number is given, it applies to all sizes.

Finished Measurement

Length: 9 (10, 11) inches

Materials

- Berroco Comfort Chunky (chunky weight; 50% super fine nylon/50% super fine acrylic; 150 yds/100g per ball): 2 balls hummus #5720
- Size 10 (6mm) double-point needles or size needed to obtain gauge
- Cable needle
- Stitch marker
- 12-inch square of 1-inch high-density foam

Gauge

17 sts and 20 rows = 4 inches/10cm in St st. To save time, take time to check gauge.

House of White Birches, Berne, Indiana 46711   AnniesAttic.com

Special Techniques

Make 1 (M1): Insert LH needle from front to back under strand between the last st worked and next st on LH needle, k1-tbl.

Cable 4 back (C4B): Slip next 2 sts onto cn and hold to back, k2, k2 from cn.

Cable 4 front (C4F): Slip next 2 sts onto cn and hold to front, k2, k2 from cn.

Pattern Stitch

Horseshoe Cable (panel of 20 sts)

Row 1 (RS): P2, k4, C4B, C4F, k4, p2.

Rows 2 and 4: K2, p16, k2.

Row 3: P2, k2, C4B, k4, C4F, k2, p2.

Row 5: P2, C4B, k8, C4F, p2.

Row 6: K2, p16, k2.

Rep Rows 1–6 for pat.

Pattern Notes

Two double-point needles are used to work back and forth in rows on the smaller number of stitches used for slippers.

Work increases and decreases 1 stitch in from each edge.

Slipper

Sole

Make 2 per slipper

Cast on 7 sts.

Work 2 rows even in St st.

Continue in St st, inc 1 st by M1 at each end [every other row] twice—11 sts.

Work even until piece measures 3 (3½, 4) inches from beg.

Inc 1 st at each end [every 4th row] 3 times—17 sts.

Work even until piece measures 8 (9, 10) inches.

Dec 1 st each end by k1, ssk, work to last 3 sts, k2tog, k1 [every other row] 3 times—11 sts.

Bind off.

Toe

Cast on 20 sts.

Row 1 (RS): P2, k2, p2, k8, p2, k2, p2.

Row 2: K2, p2, k2, p8, k2, p2, k2.

Rep Rows 1 and 2 until toe measures 1 inch, ending with a WS row.

Work Rows 1–6 of Horseshoe Cable pat until toe measures 4 (4½, 5) inches.

Continue in pat, dec 1 st at each end [every other row] 3 times—14 sts.

Bind off.

Finishing

Block pieces. Trace shape of sole on high-density foam, cut out 1 piece for each slipper.

Side Trim

Cast on 4 sts. Work in St st for approx 23 (25, 27) inches, or distance around outside edge of foam. Bind off.

For each slipper, sandwich foam between 2 sole pieces. Pin side trim in place around side edge of foam. Sew top sole to 1 long edge of side trim, and bottom sole to other long edge of side trim, enclosing foam.

Sew toe in place at top of sole. ❖

Mitered Square Scuffs

Design by Amy Polcyn

Skill Level

 ☐☐ EASY

Sizes

Woman's small (medium, large) Fits shoe size 5–7 (8–10, 11–13) Instructions are given for smallest size with larger sizes in parentheses. When only 1 number is given it applies to all sizes.

Finished Measurement

Length: 9 (10, 11) inches

Materials

- Aslan Trends Kettle Dyed Bariloche (worsted weight; 85% wool/ 15% polyamide; 175 yds/100g per skein): 1 (2, 2) skein(s) grape jam #1319
- Size 8 (5mm) double-point needles or size needed to obtain gauge
- Size G/6 (4mm) crochet hook
- Stitch marker
- Super heavy weight interfacing (such as Timtex) or stiffened felt

4 MEDIUM

Gauge

18 sts and 36 rows = 4 inches/10cm in garter st. To save time, take time to check gauge.

Special Abbreviations

Central Double Decrease (CDD): Slip next 2 sts as if to k2tog, k1, pass 2 slipped sts over the knit st and off the needle.

Knit in front and back (kfb): Inc by knitting in front and then in back of next st.

Pattern Note

Two double-point needles are used to work back and forth in rows on the smaller number of stitches used for these slippers.

Work increases and decreases on sole 1 stitch in from each edge.

Slipper

Sole

Make 2 per slipper

Cast on 8 sts.

Work 2 rows even in garter st.

Continue in garter st, inc 1 st by kfb at each end [every other row] twice—12 sts.

Work even in garter st until piece measures 4 (5, 6) inches from beg.

Inc 1 st at each end [every 4th row] 3 times—18 sts.

Work even until piece measures 7 (8, 9) inches.

Dec 1 st at each end [every other row] 8 times—2 sts.

Bind off.

Toe

Cast on 27 sts. Place marker on center st.

Row 1 (RS): Knit.

Row 2: Knit to 1 st before marker, CDD; knit to end of row.

Rep Rows 1 and 2 until 3 sts rem.

Next row: K3tog—1 st. Fasten off.

Hold square on point, with RS facing and cast-on edges at top. Pick up and knit 13 sts along one cast-on side.

Row 1 (WS): Knit.

Row 2: Ssk, knit to last 2 sts, k2tog.

Rep Rows 1 and 2 until 3 sts rem.

Next row: K3tog—1 st. Fasten off.

Rep on other cast-on side of square. Piece is now a pentagon shape.

Note: Original cast-on edge, where sts have just been added, is the lower edge of the toe.

Finishing

Trace sole shape on interfacing or felt, cut out 2 pieces. For each slipper, sandwich 1 interfacing piece between 2 sole pieces. With crochet hook, work 1 rnd of sc around edge of sole, enclose interfacing.

Sc across lower edge of toe. Position toe piece on sole and sc around edge of toe joining it to sole. ❖

Ruggedly Warm Loafers

Design by Amy Polcyn

Skill Level

⬛⬛⬛◻ **INTERMEDIATE**

Sizes

Unisex small (medium, large) Fits shoe sizes 7–9 (10–12, 13+) Instructions are given for smallest size, with larger sizes in parentheses. When only 1 number is given, it applies to all sizes.

Finished Measurement

Length: 10 (11, 12) inches

Materials

- Berroco Sundae super bulky (super chunky weight; 50% wool/50% acrylic; 62 yds/100g per hank): 2 hanks stilton #8717
- Size 11 (8mm) double-point needles
- Size 13 (9mm) double-point needles or size needed to obtain gauge
- Stitch marker

Gauge

10 sts and 14 rows = 4 inches/10cm in St st on larger needles.
To save time, take time to check gauge.

Special Technique
Wrap and Turn (W/T): Work to st indicated, *on RS rows*, bring yarn between needles to front of work, slip next st to RH needle, take yarn to back, slip wrapped st back to LH needle and turn; *on WS rows*, take yarn between needles to back, slip next st to RH needle, bring yarn between needles to front, slip wrapped st back to LH needle and turn.

Pattern Notes
Two double-point needles are used to work back and forth in rows on the smaller number of stitches used for the heel, foot and toe of slippers.

Top edge is worked in rounds with the set of double-point needles.

Loafer
With larger needles, cast on 12 sts.

Heel
Work short-row heel in St st as follows:

Row 1 (RS): Knit to last st, W/T.

Row 2: Purl to last st, W/T.

Row 3: Knit to last 2 sts, W/T.

Row 4: Purl to last 2 sts, W/T.

Row 5: Knit to last 3 sts, W/T.

Row 6: Purl to last 3 sts, W/T.

Row 7: Knit to last 4 sts, W/T.

Row 8: Purl to last 4 sts, W/T.

Note: There are 4 wrapped sts at each end of row and 4 unwrapped sts in the center.

Row 9: Sl 1p, knit to first wrapped st (4th stitch from end of row), lift wrap and knit tog with wrapped st, turn.

Row 10: Sl 1p, purl to first wrapped st (4th stitch from end of row), lift wrap and purl tog with wrapped st, turn.

Row 11: Sl 1p, knit to wrapped st, lift wrap and knit tog with wrapped st, turn.

Row 12: Sl 1p, purl to wrapped st, lift wrap and purl tog with wrapped st, turn.

Continue in same manner until all wrapped sts have been worked.

Foot
Work even in St st until piece measures 8 (9, 10) inches.

Note: Measure length in center of row.

Toe
Work same as heel until all wrapped sts have been worked. Bind off.

Top Edge
Beg at center back, with smaller needles, pick up and knit 50 (54, 58) sts evenly around top. Place marker and join to work in rnds.

Rnd 1: Purl.

Rnd 2: Knit.

Rnd 3: Purl.

Bind off kwise.

Toe edge ribbing
With smaller needles and RS facing, pick up and knit 11 sts across toe.

Next row (WS): *P1-tbl, k1; rep from * across to last st, p1-tbl.

Next row (RS): *K1-tbl, p1; rep from * across to last st, k1-tbl.

Rep last 2 rows for 2 inches. Bind off in pat.

Finishing
Sew side edges of ribbing to top edges. ❖

Easy Zip Slippers

Design by Amy Polcyn

Skill Level
 ■■□□ EASY

Sizes
Man's small (medium, large) Fits shoe sizes 7–9 (10–12, 13+) Instructions are given for smallest size, with larger sizes in parentheses. When only 1 number is given, it applies to all sizes.

Finished Measurement
Length: 10 (11, 12) inches

Materials
- TLC Heathers (worsted weight; 100% acrylic; 260 yds/141g per skein): 1 skein nutmeg #2443
- Size 9 (5.5mm) double-point needles or size needed to obtain gauge
- Stitch marker
- 2 (7-inch) zippers
- Sewing needle and matching thread

Gauge
16 sts and 32 rows = 4 inches/10cm in garter st. To save time, take time to check gauge.

Pattern Note
Two double-point needles are used to work back and forth in rows on the smaller number of stitches used for the heel, foot and toe of slippers.

Slipper
Cast on 20 sts.

Heel
Work origami heel in garter st as follows:

Rows 1 (RS) and 2: Sl 1p, knit to last st, turn.

Rows 3 and 4: Sl 1p, knit to last 2 sts, turn.

Rows 5 and 6: Sl 1p, knit to last 3 sts, turn.

Rows 7 and 8: Sl 1p, knit to last 4 sts, turn.

Rows 9 and 10: Sl 1p, knit to last 5 sts, turn.

Rows 11 and 12: Sl 1p, knit to last 6 sts, turn.

Note: There are now 6 unworked sts at each end and 8 sts in the center.

Next row (RS): Sl 1p, knit to last 6 sts, pick up st from row below (as for a lifted increase) and work as ssk tog with next st on needle.

Next row: Sl 1p, knit to last 6 sts, pick up st from row below and k2tog with next st on needle.

Next row: Sl 1p, knit to last 5 sts, pick up st from row below and ssk tog with next st on needle.

Next row: Sl 1p, knit to last 5 sts, pick up st from row below and k2tog with next st on needle.

Continue as established until all sts have been worked.

Foot
Work even in garter st until piece measures 8 (9, 10) inches.

Toe
Work same as heel.

Work even in garter st for 2½ (3, 3½) inches. Bind off.

Sew sides of toe flap in place on sides of slipper.

Top
With RS facing, beg at center of toe, pick up and knit 58 (62, 66) sts around top of slipper. Do not join. Work back and forth in rows in garter st.

Row 1 (RS): K1, ssk, knit to last 3 sts, k2tog, k1.

Row 2: Knit.

Rep Rows 1 and 2 until 40 sts rem.

Work even until piece measures 3 inches above last dec row. Bind off.

Finishing

Measure desired length for zipper, shortening if necessary, following package instructions. Pin zipper in place, sew with needle and thread. ❖

Standard Abbreviations

[ ] work instructions within brackets as many times as directed

( ) work instructions within parentheses in the place directed

** repeat instructions following the asterisks as directed

 * repeat instructions following the single asterisk as directed

 " inch(es)

approx approximately

beg begin/begins/beginning

CC contrasting color

ch chain stitch

cm centimeter(s)

cn cable needle

dec decrease/decreases/ decreasing

dpn(s) double-point needle(s)

g gram(s)

inc increase/increases/increasing

k knit

k2tog knit 2 stitches together

kwise knitwise

LH left hand

m meter(s)

M1 make one stitch

MC main color

mm millimeter(s)

oz ounce(s)

p purl

pat(s) pattern(s)

p2tog purl 2 stitches together

psso pass slipped stitch over

p2sso pass 2 slipped stitches over

pwise purlwise

rem remain/remains/remaining

rep repeat(s)

rev St st reverse stockinette stitch

RH right hand

rnd(s) round(s)

RS right side

skp slip, knit, pass slipped stitch over— one stitch decreased

sk2p slip 1, knit 2 together, pass slip stitch over the knit 2 together —2 stitches have been decreased

sl slip

sl 1k slip 1 knitwise

sl 1p slip 1 purlwise

sl st slip stitch(es)

ssk slip, slip, knit these 2 stitches together —a decrease

st(s) stitch(es)

St st stockinette stitch/ stocking stitch

tbl through back loop(s)

tog together

WS wrong side

wyib with yarn in back

wyif with yarn in front

yd(s) yard(s)

yfwd yarn forward

yo yarn over

Standard Yarn Weight System

Categories of yarn, gauge ranges, and recommended needle sizes

Yarn Weight Symbol & Category Names	 SUPER FINE	FINE	LIGHT	MEDIUM	BULKY	SUPER BULKY
Type of Yarns in Category	Sock, Fingering, Baby	Sport, Baby	DK, Light Worsted	Worsted, Afghan, Aran	Chunky, Craft, Rug	Super Chunky, Roving
Knit Gauge Range* in Stockinette Stitch to 4 inches	27–32 sts	23–26 sts	21–24 sts	16–20 sts	12–15 sts	6–11 sts
Recommended Needle in Metric Size Range	2.25–3.25mm	3.25–3.75mm	3.75–4.5mm	4.5–5.5mm	5.5–8mm	8mm and larger
Recommended Needle U.S. Size Range	1 to 3	3 to 5	5 to 7	7 to 9	9 to 11	11 and larger

* GUIDELINES ONLY: The above reflect the most commonly used gauges and needle sizes for specific yarn categories.

House of White Birches, Berne, Indiana 46711   AnniesAttic.com

Knitting Basics

Cast-On

Leaving an end about an inch long for each stitch to be cast on, make a slip knot on the right needle.

Place the thumb and index finger of your left hand between the yarn ends with the long yarn end over your thumb, and the strand from the skein over your index finger. Close your other fingers over the strands to hold them against your palm. Spread your thumb and index fingers apart and draw the yarn into a "V."

Place the needle in front of the strand around your thumb and bring it underneath this strand. Carry the needle over and under the strand on your index finger.

Draw through loop on thumb.

Drop the loop from your thumb and draw up the strand to form a stitch on the needle.

Repeat until you have cast on the number of stitches indicated in the pattern. Remember to count the beginning slip knot as a stitch.

Cable Cast-On

This type of cast-on is used when adding stitches in the middle or at the end of a row.

Make a slip knot on the left needle. Knit a stitch in this knot and place it on the left needle. Insert the right needle between the last two stitches on the left needle. Knit a stitch and place it on the left needle. Repeat for each stitch needed.

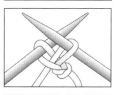

Knit (k)

Insert tip of right needle from front to back in next stitch on left needle.

Bring yarn under and over the tip of the right needle.

Pull yarn loop through the stitch with right needle point.

Slide the stitch off the left needle. The new stitch is on the right needle.

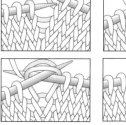

Purl (p)

With yarn in front, insert tip of right needle from back to front through next stitch on the left needle.

Bring yarn around the right needle counterclockwise. With right needle, draw yarn back through the stitch.

Slide the stitch off the left needle. The new stitch is on the right needle.

Bind-Off

Binding off (knit)

Knit first two stitches on left needle. Insert tip of left needle into first stitch worked on right needle and pull it over the second stitch and completely off the needle.

Knit the next stitch and repeat. When one stitch remains on right needle, cut yarn and draw tail through last stitch to fasten off.

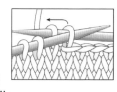

Binding off (purl)

Purl first two stitches on left needle. Insert tip of left needle into first stitch worked on right needle and pull it over the second stitch and completely off the needle.

Purl the next stitch and repeat. When one stitch remains on right needle, cut yarn and draw tail through last stitch to fasten off.

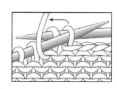

Increase (inc)

Two stitches in one stitch

Increase (knit)
Knit the next stitch in the usual manner, but don't remove the stitch from the left needle. Place right needle behind left needle and knit again into the back of the same stitch. Slip original stitch off left needle.

Increase (purl)
Purl the next stitch in the usual manner, but don't remove the stitch from the left needle. Place right needle behind left needle and purl again into the back of the same stitch. Slip original stitch off left needle.

Invisible Increase (M1)
There are several ways to make or increase one stitch.

Make 1 with Left Twist (M1L)
Insert left needle from front to back under the horizontal loop between the last stitch worked and next stitch on left needle.

With right needle, knit into the back of this loop.

To make this increase on the purl side, insert left needle in same manner and purl into the back of the loop.

Make 1 with Right Twist (M1R)
Insert left needle from back to front under the horizontal loop between the last stitch worked and next stitch on left needle.

With right needle, knit into the front of this loop.

To make this increase on the purl side, insert left needle in same manner and purl into the front of the loop.

Make 1 with Backward Loop over the right needle
With your thumb, make a loop over the right needle.

Slip the loop from your thumb onto the needle and pull to tighten.

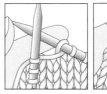

Make 1 in top of stitch below
Insert tip of right needle into the stitch on left needle one row below.

Knit this stitch, then knit the stitch on the left needle.

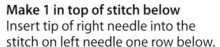

Decrease (dec)
Knit 2 together (k2tog)
Put tip of right needle through next two stitches on left needle as to knit. Knit these two stitches as one.

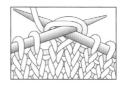

Purl 2 together (p2tog)
Put tip of right needle through next two stitches on left needle as to purl. Purl these two stitches as one.

Slip, Slip, Knit (ssk)
Slip next two stitches, one at a time, as to knit from left needle to right needle.

Insert left needle in front of both stitches and work off needle together.

Slip, Slip, Purl (ssp)
Slip next two stitches, one at a time, as to knit from left needle to right needle. Slip these stitches back onto left needle keeping them twisted. Purl these two stitches together through back loops.

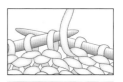

House of White Birches, Berne, Indiana 46711 AnniesAttic.com

Single Crochet (sc)

Insert hook in stitch (a), yarn over, draw loop through (b), yarn over, draw through both loops on hook (c).

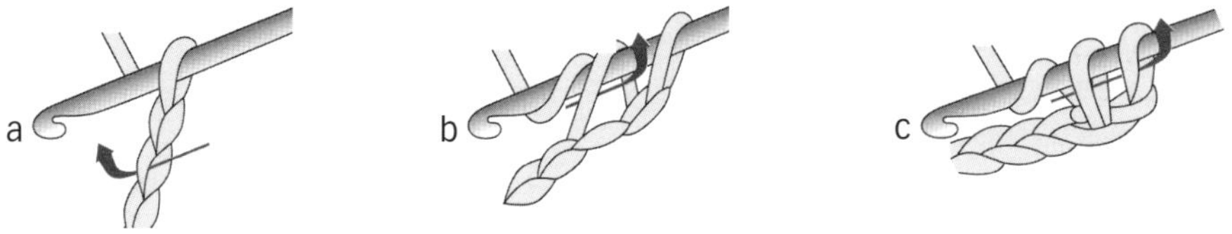

Knitting Needle Conversion Chart

U.S.	1	2	3	4	5	6	7	8	9	10	10½	11	13	15	17	19	35	50
Continental-mm	2.25	2.75	3.25	3.5	3.75	4	4.5	5	5.5	6	6.5	8	9	10	12	15	19	25

Inches into Millimetres & Centimetres

All measurements are rounded off slightly.

inches	mm	cm	inches	cm	inches	cm	inches	cm	inches	cm
⅛	3	0.3	3	7.5	13	33.0	26	66.0	39	99.0
¼	6	0.6	3½	9.0	14	35.5	27	68.5	40	101.5
⅜	10	1.0	4	10.0	15	38.0	28	71.0	41	104.0
½	13	1.3	4½	11.5	16	40.5	29	73.5	42	106.5
⅝	15	1.5	5	12.5	17	43.0	30	76.0	43	109.0
¾	20	2.0	5½	14	18	46.0	31	79.0	44	112.0
⅞	22	2.2	6	15.0	19	48.5	32	81.5	45	114.5
1	25	2.5	7	18.0	20	51.0	33	84.0	46	117.0
1¼	32	3.8	8	20.5	21	53.5	34	86.5	47	119.5
1½	38	3.8	9	23.0	22	56.0	35	89.0	48	122.0
1¾	45	4.5	10	25.5	23	58.5	36	91.5	49	124.5
2	50	5.0	11	28.0	24	61.0	37	94.0	50	127.0
2½	65	6.5	12	30.5	25	63.5	38	96.5		

Skill Levels

BEGINNER

Beginner projects for first-time knitters using basic stitches. Minimal shaping.

EASY

Easy projects using basic stitches, repetitive stitch patterns, simple color changes, and simple shaping and finishing.

INTERMEDIATE

Intermediate projects with a variety of stitches, mid-level shaping and finishing.

EXPERIENCED

Experienced projects using advanced techniques and stitches, detailed shaping and refined finishing.

Meet the Designer

Amy Polcyn

Amy has been designing professionally since 2005. Her work appears regularly in major knitting magazines and in yarn company pattern collections. She loves designing projects that are simple to knit with an interesting twist, such as cables, unusual construction or a bit of colorwork. In addition to designing, Amy works as a technical editor for yarn companies, magazines and independent designers. Prior to casting off her day job for a full-time career in fiber, she worked for 10 years as an elementary teacher in a school for gifted students. Amy lives in suburban Detroit with her husband of 15 years, 10 year-old daughter and 2 wool-loving cats. In her spare time, Amy enjoys bellydance, long walks and spending as much time as possible with her spinning wheel.

HOUSE of WHITE BIRCHES
PUBLISHERS SINCE 1947

Knit a Dozen Plus Slippers is published by DRG, 306 East Parr Road, Berne, IN 46711. Printed in USA. Copyright © 2010 DRG. All rights reserved. This publication may not be reproduced in part or in whole without written permission from the publisher.

RETAIL STORES: If you would like to carry this pattern book or any other DRG publications, visit DRGwholesale.com

Every effort has been made to ensure that the instructions in this pattern book are complete and accurate. We cannot, however, take responsibility for human error, typographical mistakes or variations in individual work. Please visit AnniesCustomerCare.com to check for pattern updates.

ISBN: 978-1-59217-302-0

3 4 5 6 7 8 9

Photo Index

7

10

19

13

16

22

25

28

31

34

37

4

40